This book is dedicated to the research scholars who make their study on Bharati Mukherjee with reference to the women character and their plight.

BI-CULTURALISM: AN IMPACT ON FEMALE IDENTITY

WITH REFERENCE TO BHARATI MUKHERJEE'S 'TARA, DIMPLE, JASMINE'

DR. M DIVYA

Copyright © Dr. M Divya
All Rights Reserved.

This book has been self-published with all reasonable efforts taken to make the material error-free by the author. No part of this book shall be used, reproduced in any manner whatsoever without written permission from the author, except in the case of brief quotations embodied in critical articles and reviews.

The Author of this book is solely responsible and liable for its content including but not limited to the views, representations, descriptions, statements, information, opinions and references ["Content"]. The Content of this book shall not constitute or be construed or deemed to reflect the opinion or expression of the Publisher or Editor. Neither the Publisher nor Editor endorse or approve the Content of this book or guarantee the reliability, accuracy or completeness of the Content published herein and do not make any representations or warranties of any kind, express or implied, including but not limited to the implied warranties of merchantability, fitness for a particular purpose. The Publisher and Editor shall not be liable whatsoever for any errors, omissions, whether such errors or omissions result from negligence, accident, or any other cause or claims for loss or damages of any kind, including without limitation, indirect or consequential loss or damage arising out of use, inability to use, or about the reliability, accuracy or sufficiency of the information contained in this book.

Made with ♥ on the Notion Press Platform
www.notionpress.com

Contents

Foreword *vii*

Preface *ix*

Acknowledgements *xi*

1. Bi-culturalism: An Overview 1

2. Bi-culturalism: An Impact On Female Identity 19

Bibliography 43

Foreword

The book takes both the concepts of diaspora and immigration together exploring the dynamics of post-colonial cultural identity. This study takes up the definition of the term 'self' of women. 'Self' is nothing but an inner urge which springs from instinct, and stimulates thinking. Self depends upon the mind-sets also. The issues that the protagonists face being an immigrant play a vital role in reconstructing identity. In society, women struggle to bring out their identity because of the male dominance. Besides, they suffer the cultural changes happen due to the advent of the post- colonialism.

Dr.R.Sudha, Assistant Professor of English

Preface

The book discuss some aspects of post colonialism, biculturalism, immigration and the politics of identity with specific relevance to the issues of female identity. The book also holds up for view and analyses Bharati Mukherjee's perspectives on the demystification of identity with particular relevance to the novels undertaken for the analysis. The book renders a brief overview of post-colonial theory and its praxis keeping in view the particularities of the issues of identity and a critical perspective on Bharati Mukherjee's approach to the issue of immigration and bi-culturalism, its impact on identity reconstruction in the modern society and necessary narratives as a whole. However, the transformation of Bharati Mukherjee as a writer and a dweller of the new world happened with the act of immigration in the United States in 1980.

Acknowledgements

I thank God Almighty for giving me the strength, knowledge, ability and opportunity to undertake this project. My sincere thanks to PSG College of Arts and Science, Coimbatore, India for the constant support rendered to complete the book harmoniously. I'm extreemly thankful to my editor Dr.R.Sudha for her mediculous effort.

ONE

Bi-Culturalism: An Overview

In respect of the social science, identity takes a vital role in the character of the women. So, the novelist takes much interest not only in the observation of the women's behaviour and social dignity but also in the perception of the bio- cultural attitude and transnational involvement of the immigrant characters. Self- expression is an outcome of self- depression. In the case of the women who live in the modern society, suffer from the psyche splits personality. Owing to the biculturalism, the so called the protagonists are left in the middle course with oscillating thought action. However, the women characters Tara, Dimple or Jasmine or anybody else who want to settle down in the US inevitably embrace biculturalism so as to demystify their self- irrespective of caste, creed or religion.

The women like the protagonists suffer for want of freedom and they are portrayed as the woman who is so anxious to demystify the identity. Out of the diasporic experiences, they encounter transformation and new environmental survival. Instead of the Indian tradition, the immigrant characters become victim to the Americanization because of fascination with deep- rooted western culture. At times, the married women oscillate to keep up their social dignity and identity which are the best traits for the integrity of their personality. Though women confuse themselves, the self (inner urge or oracle) makes them go forward in a right direction. Never have they liked to be against destiny. Ultimately they are ambitious of keeping up identity in the society where they are totally ignored.

Not only the post-colonial theory but the biculturalism needs an analysis of these practices represented by discussion in which identity of the female characters is considered as important feature of this book. Because culture is a mobile signifier that enables distinct ways of talking about human activity. Identity speaks about the points of temporary attachment to the subject positions which discursive practices construct for us.

The identity of the post-colonial "third world" immigrant evolves out of the strategic identifications pertaining to class, ethnicity, gender, sexuality, race, language, culture, homeland or adopted land, locality or community, time and space. In the transculture global age, the important facet of cultural identity of the women is in being what she wants her to be. The results of the colonial experience are tragic. Identity is not conventional; it changes its course in displacement. It can be changed. It implies challenge besides integrity and dignity. Identity is the mainspring of destiny. It comes due to the mutation and fascination of the new environment.

It is true that diaspora identity produces and reproduces itself anew, through transformation and marginalization. Post-colonial identity is a rope of the contemporary future as seen by theorists like Arjun Appadurai, JungenHabermas , Donold Peese and Manuel Castells.

As far as American mainstream is concerned, the Indian diaspora is one of the ethnic categories which continually reshape to form its composite culture or cultural syncretism. As the limits of this thesis are confined to the cultural encounter of the protagonists as Indian immigrants with the American culture as reflected in the novels of Bharati Mukherjee, this thesis will focus on acculturation with reference to the Indian Americans interacting with the American mainstream.

The process of adapting to the American mainstream strikes the root of the phenomenal transnationalism, the advantage of Globalization and technology. Cultural studies associated with the post-colonial theory draws our attention to the thesis. Since migration is synonymous with mobility, there arises an inevitability of constructing culturalism of the immigrant community where the women take much effort and enthusiasm to bring out their identity. The book employs the concept of bicultural construction and psychological transformation that would justify the title.

The book signifies the murders that are committed by the characters in the novel. The writer has attempted to emphasize the injustices by men and women who contemplate murdering someone. Murdering someone can never become ones identity in fact it is inhuman and evil. The illustrations given by the novelist seems to be admirable. The approach to culture echoes an anti-essential perspective on identity is dealt in the novel. In the novels taken up for the study, there emerges a conscious involvement and engagement in the reconstruction of cultural and ideological representation too. For such interrogations this thesis harnesses the methodology and approach of both post-colonial theory and cultural studies. This facilitates the exploration of the dynamics of reinterpretation of culture and impact by Bharati Mukherjee's immigrant characters in the process of their identity-demystification. The relocation context covers as mentioned, the United States of America.

Bharati Mukherjee revives her interest in her fiction and describes expatriation, transformation of identity, cultural conflicts with their respective impacts upon the immigrant psyche and socio- cultural economic problems of adjustment of the new environment in the new land. Mukherjee particularises to say that the immigrant women could hardly follow traditional values of their home land while staying
in the host land. Above all, Mukherjee expresses her willingness to adopt the concept of marginalisation in the context of the immigrant women to the 'Receiver society'. In the view of Bharati Mukherjee, immigration is a process of profit in contrast to loss in transit to a new culture. Apparently, it is said to be a gain for the female characters who prefer individual identity to the communal identity.
The individual identity that transforms and evolves Jasmine, Tara and Dimple reconstruct their identities extremely well. It is found that her narrative voice undergoes transformation, changing socio- cultural and political scene of immigration in the U.S.A.

Bharati Mukherjee's immigrant female protagonists are drawn either from the middle class or from the upper class Indian family. The characters are mostly affected with the dilemmas of identity transformation and choices at their disposal. 'Self' of the female characters makes us aware that there is a 'fighting within'. The identification may be a deliberate or unconscious act but this is a venue where Mukherjee's identity exposition comes into play. She creates her characters with choices of agency and transformation, believing in the workings of fate.

Not only narratives but also sub- narratives receive indistinguishable significance compact with passion and metaphors of the artist's observation of life, history, nation, culture, delineation and above all the art of indirection over Mukherjee writing. Referring to the First world and Third World confirms us that she has literary acumen with history too.

Bharati Mukherjee does not like her novel to be the work of feminism. Her three novels are in the contexts of diaspora, biculturalism and transnationalism. Description about her homeland is structured within the myths, memories and the culture of the Indian nation. Immigrant women's movement to a new land is kept at the hybridity of in between cultures of India and America. Projecting the differences in cultures between the motherland and other land, she tries to negotiate these differences by means of using Indian mythology as responsible answers to the grand narratives of the western countries.

Bharati Mukherjee's characters aim at exposing their own identity, ethnicity and integrity. They are successful at carving out their own individuality in the New World. The novelist does not want her to be confined to the post-colonial perspective but takes much interest to illuminate biculturalism. It is proud to recall that Bharati Mukherjee is one among the female novelists who represent Indian writing in English as the representative of everything that is Indian. In representing the Third World Bharati Mukherjee echoes Frederic Jameson's contention that Third World texts are national allegories. The complexities within Third

World have to be taken into consideration class, caste, gender, sexuality. Anyhow, the post colonialists find the perpetuation of homogenization of the 'Third World' natives and the perpetuation of their marginalization in Bharati Mukherjee. For her, immigration gains momentum in her fiction. To her sense and sight, America seems to be a new world because of its fast- track modern technology, globalization, transculturation, transformation and immigration. However, it is admirable and agreeable to assure that Mukherjee still uses the terms 'New World and old world'. Certainly the novelist equates America with the new world and the immigrant women as residents of the old world.

Bharati Mukherjee being an Indian born American novelist occupies a unique position among the contemporary literary writers. She is called as the 'foremost chronicler of the multicultural new America'. In an interview with Bharati Mukherjee, she openly admits as follows because the female characters projected by the novelist in these novels come across so many immigrant, diasporic experiences and biculturalism. Struggle for identity- exposition is favourable as well as admirable because the female characters brave the new environment in the form of destiny. However, their attempt never becomes futile to show their individual identity in the society.

The modern woman like Tara or Dimple or Jasmine, do not find any sense in self-sacrifice but she yearns for self-expression, individuality and self- identity. She is trying to be free from dependence of the male dominance. With the crumbling of moral and ethical values, there is an inner conflict which alone drives the modern Indian women to take shelter in different identities for a momentary solace.

The female characters are shown as immigrants. The immigrants alienated from their homeland, people and family feel the wrench of separation. Like Tara, any woman longs to be back to her motherland, yearning for the security and identity. What happens to Tara? Curiosity occurs in everyone's mind. Woman like her is not recognised in her motherland but she is confident of advocating identity with her American husband.

In fact, social empowerment provides the skills and the opportunities for women to use their collective power and keep up their identity with liberty from the men in the society. Women issues have been going on for many years. These female writers form a conviction that importance of literature is not merely in its way of saying but also in what it speaks emphatically. In the modern society, the impulse towards womanhood self and sufferings of women in the form of frustration, depression, suppression, oppression and regression results in revolution. To bring into notice of every woman, the novelists like Bharati Mukherjee contributes these novels *The Tiger's Daughter, Wife* and *Jasmine* that echo their voice for up keeping the female identity as a mark of liberty. Helena Grice reminds us: Bharati Mukherjee not only established herself as a decisive voice in the US multiculturalist debate but also consolidated her position as one of the best known South Asian American writer.

India is also a land where female goddesses are worshipped. The woman is still seen as a source of strength and life- giving source. The clash of cultures, emerging dilemmas and finally success of assimilation are the integral themes in the text of Bharati Mukherjee. The protagonists are pushed into the accessibility of these factors. To strive, to see but not to yield determine the characters and make them solve the problems of immigration, ethnic alienation in the foreign land. Since her characters embrace new culture, they feel too difficult to be free- minded.

The novelist depicts the protagonists as new immigrant women who are forced to mutate and transform themselves as self – emancipated, self – confident and self – dignified members of the American society. Tara, Dimple and Jasmine, who are Indians, never give up spirit of Americanization too. What all these women aspire is nothing but identity, liberty and equality from the men in the society. Curiosity arises and enquiry springs up from everyone's mind. Whether the women like Tara, Dimple, Jasmine achieve their aim. Readers become convinced through the attribution of the novelist that the female characters fulfil their aim through self-assertion.

The novelist interposes skilfully to uncloak the dilemma of the befuddled and bemoaned protagonists because their inner conflicts prevent them from recounting their experiences and revealing their psychological process of assimilation. Positively not only biculturalism, immigration but also transformation form a new environment for the women and throw the women into turbulence.

The female characters become agitated, aggressive and sensitive. They prepare themselves to encounter anything in the society. Their ultimate aim is to bring out their identity. The novels which are taken up for the study, expose not only the theme of inner urge do styled self in these characters but also lay stress upon the sub-themes which add to the repression of the protagonist. The characters of Mukherjee are a reflection of the unspoken truth under the face of esteemed tradition and culture. The thought process and expression of the characters bear the mark of unavoidable new situation in the patriarchal society. Besides speaking about oriental and occidental conflict cross – culturalism, the novelist deals with the downtrodden corners of the inner self which directs the characters to be in constant search for freedom and identity. The experience of one's adapting to a new society is in fact a process unique for each woman. The possibility of participating in the new or foreign society brings out the identity of any man or woman. In this connection, Jasmine, Dimple fulfil their needs.

Any woman who aspires to celebrate equal right with men because of untold sufferings attempt to prove their identity eliminating the male – chauvinism. Issues of diaspora and national identity figure prominently in her novels which have been selected for research. There is an emotional upheaval in the mind of the characters.

Bharati Mukherjee's evolution as a woman novelist is manifested in the themes of themes of three novels that she has chosen to focus on. Her journey from the cloistered environment of highly upper class Bengali Brahmin in Calcutta to the cosmopolitan world of North America is epochal. The multifarious themes executed revealed in the characters by the novelist give an impact on the reader's mind. In fact, Bharati Mukherjee portrays disharmony as well as sexual relationship of the women who are thrown into the pathetic position in the society. She assures through the characters that not only indignity but also inequality brings about the detrimental identity to their peaceful life.

It is a challenge for the women who try to come out of the complexity and confusion of life because of embarrassment and embracing of biculturalism. Without art, there would in no way be of knowing where the world is moving or what the meaning and the purpose of life is all about. Bharati Mukherjee understands the crisis of the women in the society and relates their respective character for the women. The sole aim of the novelist is to find remedy for the women, sufferers of the society through art and literature. So, she has contributed three novels which highlight the ideals of democracy and freedom of the individual. Humanity gets influenced in the characterization. Praise goes to Mukherjee's work that centres on the confidence, assertiveness or subversiveness of her female characters like Tara, Dimple and Jasmine.

Bharati Mukherjee, in *Wife* , highlights the marginalization of women by exploring and exploding ways in which culture and ideology construct feminine identity, with the help of a constantly evolving imagination, like her fictional characters, the novelist looks forward not for the present reality. With emphatic tone, she feels the reinvention of self instead of nostalgia. Self – assertion empowers the women to achieve something else beyond marginalization.

A sense of isolation and transformation forces a woman to find out an alternative within her that will be a stronghold of her own identity. In jasmine, the characters as immigrant take roles in the dominant culture. The potential of fluidity which Bharati Mukherjee attributes to America's culture is epitomised in the major characters' metamorphosis from Jyothi, a Punjabi village girl to Jasmine, a loving and devoted Hindu wife to Kali, incarnation of destroying Goddess to Jazzy a recreated non – immigrant to Jase, a nanny in the home of New York College professor and to Jane live in partner of a bank official in Iowa. The women writer explores the multiple self-reinventions because of displacement. The major themes of the novelist are immigration to the west, psychological transformation and the violence, women's perspective and search for autonomy and a hybrid widow that relies on her Hindu roots, Americanization and increasingly on transnationalism.

The protagonist in each novel through violent act, transform themselves to live with own identity they wish to be in the New World. Manifestation of self-empowerment is in the hands of the women. Another motif from Hinduism an integral part of the female protagonists is nothing but self – realization of their 'power' either through rebellion or regression. The Indian American novelist signifies herself in the American status, with social, economical and cultural realities. The novel shows the cross cultured metamorphosis of the female protagonists. The ultimate aim of the novelist is to recover her lost identity and understand psyche – impact through female characters, Tara, Dimple and Jasmine.

One can find out the combination of the traditional Hindu culture with the New American culture gives an impact to each of her novels. In fact, these novels bear evidences of the novelist's awareness of the various problems and issues pertaining to the women that arise from purely psychological complication. Bharati Mukherjee takes a role of neutral observer in her novels. Both defects and effects of both East and West can be found in her contributions. Her total attitude, being a novelist, is that of a reformist too. As a result of mutation, the spiritual awakening is necessary part of one's life style and it imbibes the code of ethics also. The spiritual spirit and awakening to realize the women's 'Self' are commonly infused into the structure of Mukherjee's novels with subtlety of religion that is considered as an integral part of India. The philosophies of Hinduism and Buddhism also reflect the doctrine of 'Karma' being the primeval factor in an individual's life. The philosophies drive the characters (women) to their self – realization and self – emancipation with little traditional values. Karma motivates the female characters and activates the mind and spirit to commit sin so as to expose their identity and autonomy. That is what the novelist narrates through the female characters like Tara in *The Tiger's Daughter*, Dimple in *Wife* and Jasmine in *Jasmine.*

The women are left in the middle course on account of the biculturalism which directs them all along. Despite, they mould boldness to face everything with moral support. Colonialism takes a vital role in the history of culture. It has deep rootedness. The Indian social structure became more rigid and formal in order to build psychological and metaphysical defences against colonialism. Bharati Mukherjee is entirely familiar with the interaction of the Eastern and the Western cultures and there arises a resultant identity crisis. The women's quest for their true identity in the context of cultural changes of Bharati Mukherjee stands prominent. It becomes a serious concern too.

Tara in *The Tiger's Daughter* finds it difficult to relate herself to her family, city, culture in general since her marriage with an American happened. She is branded as an alienated westernized Indian woman. Immigration one way or other initiates a sense of loss followed by the clash of bicultural and diasporic experiences. The diversity of Indian culture has a direct role to involve with the complexities of Indian women. There is no social stability in India. Women are becoming victims of patriarchal suppressions, exploitation, marginalization and multiculturalism. Tara who marries an American visits India after seven years.

As her kith and kin have absorbed with Indian traditional values, they never welcome Tara who has become Americanized. Why don't the relatives respect Tara? She has broken the Indian tradition and married David, an American against the wishes of their orthodox parents.

Bharati Mukherjee reminds one of foreignness of Tara "in India she felt she was not married to a person but to a foreigner and this foreignness was a burden" (*TD* 62). It gave a great impact to Tara who adheres to the biculturalism. She feels alienated in company of her mother. She is afraid of exposing her identity to her relatives only. On returning to her motherland, she finds grief – stricken life of the Indians in India. This sight and plight of the pathetic living of Indians touches her heart very deeply. As Tara has accustomed with assimilation and acculturation in the U.S.A,. she does not like everything in India. Tara is in remorse for having come to India. She feels that her womanhood self gets but it encourages her to her identity of Indian woman with her husband, an American. So, she makes up her mind to go back to America to her husband whom she confesses to love deeply.

Tara's visit to the funeral pyre with Tuntunwala, the sight of a girl suffering from leprosy, the pathetic scene of beggars and parentless children on the streets of Calcutta, the labours' strikes and riots prevailing in the city, Tara's declination towards the behavioural attitude of her friends and relatives, the open violence in Calcutta and molestation of Tara by Tuntunwala – these notorious incidents bring out conflicts and trauma of Tara. The change in Tara's perspective due to her Americanization is challenging for her. Generally she feels hatred for the dual standards of Indian people. Tara's faith in Indian culture becomes shattered. Tara's traditional experience makes her think about both the cultures of India and U.S.A where she finds that India culture rich in customs and traditions and never has she lost her spirit in exposing her identity even with American. Mukherjee in the role of Tara is aware of the fact that there is a dark side in respect of a women issues in the world but she takes much interest to portray the protagonists like Tara who faces the society with adaptation of both cultures and tries to bring out self – assertion and thinking that she should get due recognition and identity from her husband only.

Next contribution to *The Tiger's Daughter* is *Wife*, another novel. The central theme of the novel hangs upon the subject of marriage. Mukherjee's strong faith upon reincarnation is admirable. She has deep knowledge and attachment with Hinduism. Marriage between Dimple and Amit happens. Dimple like every other Indian girl reams about her marriage that would bring peace of mind and luxurious life. Dimple regards marriage as a good shelter to bring her freedom and means for fulfilling her dreams in the days to come.

Her heart is full of pleasure. She begins to think our imaginative world of fantasy after her marriage. Her marriage brings about misfortune in her life. Her dream becomes futile. Dimple was in anticipation that "marriage would bring her freedom" (*TD*, 3). New life started in the U.S.A. she tries to reconcile her fantasies and desires to lead a life of big dreams with great expectations from her husband. Nothing is fulfilled. She understands that she belongs to a different culture of America. She becomes enamoured with American ways of life. She suffers from psychological crisis so called insomnia. Although she spends time in watching T.V and becomes attracted to the American cultural life, she cannot have opportunity to lead a life, she cannot have opportunity to lead a life with her husband as she wishes.

Her exposure to T.V in America urges her to commit violence. She loses balance of mind and spirit. She feels too much that she suffers in America or much similar as she suffered in India. Dimple feels nostalgic in the USA. Influence of American culture in Dimple totally changed her attitude .she attains freedom which is available to the American women. She is rebellious and ambitious of demystifying her identity in the society. The killing of her husband is out and out an outcome of her Americanization. Forgetting her Indian tradition, she commits murder and avoiding Indian conventions, she feels satisfied to complete her Americanization.

In *Jasmine*, the novelist projects Jasmine as a protagonist whose role in this novel is very impressive and effective. Jasmine appears as a triumphant woman. She rebels against the Indian traditional patriarchal practices. She is disgustful of the customs of the Indian culture. She involves with every activity very confidently. She strongly decides to do whatever she determines. She throws challenges against the age old traditions and she, therefore, essays to free herself from the restrictions too. Just like Tara and Dimple immigrate to the US, she visits America. She is a woman of dreams. She wants to enjoy the American way of life. She hardly believes the superstitions. The village turned city woman who is a widow visits the US with revolutionary idea. She is in general rebellious and adamant.

Being not interested in the patriarchy, the twenty years old pregnant widow comes to America to fulfil Prakash's last wish. The typical Indian widow lives with a crippled man Bud Ripple Meyer who is her lover. Her journey of life changes from place to place (from Punjab to California, from California to Florida, New York and Iowa) adopting the new environments, Jasmine's identity begins to change with her new names. She is christened as Jyothi, which turns into Jasmine by her husband, Prakash. From Jasmine she becomes Jazzy and Jane afterwards. Soon after her husband's pen murder, she immigrates to India from America. Unfortunately she is raped by a man named half face whom she murders at last.

Amit has been relegated to the recesses of rejected memory and the new life is looked forward to with the hope, the process of defining a new identity comes begin. To survive in the US, she gets odd jobs. She works as a caregiver for the Taylor family and lives as the wife of Bud without marriage in Iowa. Notwithstanding Jasmine in the US sways between her past Indian culture, and her present experiences of American culture, she transforms herself ably. She works as a caregiver in a professor's house . The nature of the work is to take care of the adopted child Duff.

Jasmine is shocked to see Taylor, a professor serving biscuits to her (the maid). She leaves the job and moves out of the family. She understands that moving of the family frequently is an American system of the society. Jasmine herself transforms from Indian to American way of life. It originates from Taylor's house. So she confesses, "Taylor didn't want to change me. He did not want to scour and sanitize the foreignness. My being different from Wylie on Kate did not scare him. I changed because I wanted to" (*J*, 185).

She starts her adaptation of the American culture without losing the Indian values and with inculcating the

American traits, she encounters so many conflicts.

Like any woman who thinks that life is to enjoy with pleasure, Jasmine applies this notion in action to her own 'self' who becomes a fluid identity with changing names. She is an Indian immigrant but she believes and acts as an American. She takes a crucial decision justifying her act of leaving Bud and join Taylor at the end of the story. She understands that Americanization liberates her to do whatever she stays in the US. Her heart is filled with satisfaction and saturation that she can lead a life exposing her identity in the society.

She is not least bothered about the past. Her exile from country to country gives an opportunity to demystify her identity that she has grown for long time. As for the heroines of Mukherjee, in three novels, they feel that America is a land of freedom where they can do whatever they desire and live a life of their choice in whatever style they aspire to adapt. Their sojourn in America creates a chance to follow the cultures of both nations for them. So through ways and means of the cultural dichotomy they can achieve their goals, attain freedom and maintain their own identity through boldly incubated self of the womanhood. The post colonial encounter of the Indian woman immigrant is re enacted in the First world with little violence of the colonization during 19th and 20th centuries.

It draws our attention to examine the discourse that runs through Mukherjee's fiction, the ideology and the representation. What does her narrative voice? It is clean that Mukherjee, being an immigrant writer highlights the protagonists as immigrants who express their diasporic experiences. One can be sure of the fact that Mukherjee could seldom be affected by colonial traces on identity and culture of India because Bharati Mukherjee a legend in the immigration- literature claims to be an Indian American writer.

It becomes unnecessary to consider the post coloniality of Mukherjee's writing but serious concern should be put upon the analysis of the female characters that play the role of the protagonists and her three novels: *The Tiger's Daughter*, *Wife* and *Jasmine*. Mukherjee is considered as a naturalised American citizen. Her characters appeal to our sense and mind but their action touch our hearts very deeply. Excellent contribution in the field of fiction done by Mukherjee stands incomparable and admirable. The novelist's literary works and characters are set at the very stages of post colonialism, American imperialism, European colonialism and Indian post colonialism and biculturalism..

TWO

BI-CULTURALISM: AN IMPACT ON FEMALE IDENTITY

Bharati Mukherjee's fictional world presents a pathetic picture of the various experiences of women immigrants, their cultural and psychological conflicts, struggles, traumas, trials and tribulations and the heavy price some of them had to pay in their efforts to become successful immigrants in America. The analysis of Bharati Mukherjee's fictional world from a cultural and psychological perspective demonstrates that she has addressed herself to all the issues associated with expatriate experience. By choosing her protagonists from all parts of the world, she has attempted to explore the multiplicity of this theme which is centred in their struggle to outgrow inherited values. With her evolving creative vision the canvas of her thematic concern enlarges and the complexity of cultural assimilation acquires a new dimension.

The beauty in much of her fiction lies in its being informed by her personal experiences. A peculiar sense of identification with her character lends her novels a flavour rarely found among expatriate writers. It is clearly observed that because of the discrimination of culture, way of thinking and understanding, Bharati Mukherjee's, women characters become victims of cultural and psychological conflicts. In spite of all the unpleasant shadows, she is hopeful for a harmonious assimilation. She has tried to set harmony between the mainstream majority and the immigrant minority.

Owing to the fast tract advancements, the new world will be in a strong foundation to welcome global flows of culture. As they belong to new world, they have the opportunity to encounter new frontiers and valorize the third world because it is an ideal for every woman's individual fulfillment of attaining liberty, dignity, equality and identity against the male dominance in the society because the thought of the powerful woman is very part of the culture that has devised ways to channel their superior energy.

This book to explore the narratives of the female protagonists in Bharati Mukherjee's fiction exemplifying the different stages of the acculturation in the multi-culturalism, transnation, transformation, immigration, alienation and Americanization with which they entangle for the reconstruction of the identity of course, the female characters are engaged in between two worlds(old and new world) under the diasporic circumstances. Meanwhile, the advent and impact of post colonialism gave a great change in the mind of spirit of the immigrants too. The post colonialism gives a direction which encourages them and makes them aware of facing the difficulties in the society.

Certainly power of post colonialism in the age of globalization stands cause for creating as well as celebrating the multi-culturalism.

Bharati Mukherjee suggests the inevitability of transformations as necessary requisite for serving the 'unhousement' in the process of immigration. It is true that Bharati Mukherjee's concept of immigration – acculturation has undergone many changes during this period. Most of the women establish themselves in various fields to run their life. In her novels, Bharati Mukherjee, being an Indian American novelist takes much effort, interest and energy to conceptualize the image of immigrants particularly the woman who celebrate right for their self-identity by means of striving to reinstate themselves successfully in a new world. The novelist considers the immigration as an opportunity to reflect her experience through her female characterization and seizes the same opportunity to voice her belief and right that the woman like protagonists would have ultimately release from constructive social, cultural, traditional, civilizational and religious constraints.

Most of the contemporary woman authors have opted and depicted these relationships with horror but Bharati Mukherjee celebrates and entices the women's' relationship with their exotic glamour against traditional male domination. There is no anti-imperialist in Bharati Mukherjee on the other hand, the novelist, having involved with immigrant literature, creates third world of the protagonist's.

Third world heralds that either man or woman may not be obliged either to aspire or to expose his or her individuality, identity, liberty, dignity and equality in the modern society because of the multiculturalism and

transnationalism. They want to be independent in action and thought. It is a naked truth that the woman of the third world is suffering from patriarchy and oppression. From the view of the
post-colonial work, one could come to know pretty well that Bharati Mukherjee's literary work makes us aware of the collusion with western feminist's perception of the Indian woman. She portrays the third world women characters that are the symbol of the third world regression and suppression. So, literary critics insist that the complexities within "third world" have to be taken into account: class, caste, gender and injustice. Neither western feminism nor fast track racism can pull down the woman.

Bharati Mukherjee regards the U.S.A. as a new world which teems with technology, globalization, transculturalism and broad outlook. The new world positively holds a promise of new selfhood and new battles against marginalisation of the women. Post colonialism focusses the women issues of the third world so styled new world. Involving with the vicissitude of the post colonialism, Mukherjee has become an American novelist of Indian origin.

Bharati Mukherjee can be remembered in the history of fiction as a strong voice of diaspora. Her contribution to the diasporic tradition of the contemporary world is not negligible. Her continuous experimentation from *The Tiger's daughter* leaves a body of south Asian literature thoroughly enriched by new and admirable qualities which forever delight men of the post-colonial diasporic literature. Mukherjee is a writer who faces the issue of nostalgia for one's native country and culture in the transformed globalized and civilized world squarely exploring the contradictions in her own native culture and presently delightfully a revised vision of India America, the world and the new immigrants in her fiction, the novelist describes what she calls the "hybridization" of the new America whenever she is inclined to focus through character. In this correction she proudly and defiantly announces to her American readers I an interview 'I am one of you'. She declares herself as an American in the immigrant tradition.

The immigrant women in the new world attempts to get out of the oppression and regression of the enclosed atmosphere of the past cultures, exhaust energy 'self' is defined as 'fighting within solely'. It unfolds feelings of thinking. Otherwise it is said to be 'soul- stirring' too. 'Self' recurs in the mindset of a woman who is ambitious of attaining or achieving something or fulfilling one's inner urge. The ultimate aim of fighting within solely is to expose one's identity with integrity. It is absolutely a psyche spirit. As far as 'self' is concerned, her mind stands torn apart between two conflicts: to do or not to do. According to the environment 'self' helps psychological analysis. In these novels, confrontation of cultures and conflict of thoughts fight within one another. 'Self' motivates and stimulates thinking. It tries to reconcile itself.

In *The Tiger's Daughter* Bharati Mukherjee finds the problematic areas in life of the expatriate and conceptualizes Tara's split caught between her inner and outer worlds. The experience of the post – colonial elite is completely 'bicultural'. Biculturalism is an experience of detachment. The novelist projects Tara a woman of biculturalism. In the opinion of Vijay Mishra, Mukherjee characterizes her writing about migrants not as oppositional to mainstream of America but as representing the voice of New America. Ethnology is a mode of knowing in hyper reality by which Mukherjee names (real) America and reinvents a semiotics of America ethnicity.

Tara takes possible effort to reconcile these diametrically opposite worlds in her mind and heart. She is torn between her two socio – cultural identities between anchoring in an alien soil and her nostalgic for India, home country. Therefore, she fills her heart with foreignness of spirit in the process of the fast changing identity. Afterwards, she realizes that her future does not lie in it without expatriation through mutation and transnation. However, she is helpless to refuse her Indian self and is unable to remain strong in her newly discovered American self.

Dimple in *Wife* has romantic outlooks about life. Her heart is full of Whims and Fancies. Mukherjee's protagonists are tossed at an environment of ambivalence when it comes to their identity, racism and other social regressions. While negotiating displacement, the characters are courageous to face the multicultural reality in the process of cultural differentiation and assimilation. Not only multiculturalism but also ethos with which they are involved, lead them to a struggle for a new life and divulge their 'Self'. The characters created by Bharati Mukherjee have undergone different psychological – social – cultural experiences related to the process of involving, negotiating and exchanging. Mukherjee has an uppermost concern and caution that the new identity should not suffer from marginalization and suppression from any society. For this purpose, she portrays the female protagonist with qualities such as individualism, independence, self-assertion, mental courage and decisiveness. To face anything is a feature of immigrant life.

In this connection, she characterizes her writing particularly about the migrants not as oppositional to the mainstream of America but as representing the voice of the New America. Circumstances which the female protagonist face as immigrant have left direct impact upon their lives and the consequences of immigration in the diasporic lives of Tara, Dimple and Jyothi are lead to demystify their identity, the women characters dauntlessly come out from the male – dominated society. The women characters shown as potential individuals face struggle but do not become victim to the circumstances rather they are strong enough to adapt themselves to the new environment.

The multiplicity becomes a significant plight of the characters, according to their different consciousness which contradict each other but the women characters are left certain of the nature of their identity which they grow individually. The marginal and the mainstream meet each other to enact a liminal space with new significance in Tara's situation. Tara returns home land and searches for a final release which would perhaps help her choose and prove her identity, finally getting out of the ambivalent space of liminalilty. Like Jumpha Lahiri's Mrs. Sen, Tara wants to return to her parent's home

The impurity of cultures makes Tara clear and clever to expose her own identity with integrity in mind and spirit. Their sojourn in U.S.A. gives Tara a chance to observe the cultural dichotomy of both cultures and also to choose the better one to maintain her identity because of Americanization and spirit to balance the values and tradition of the past culture with the present one.

The women characters of Bharati Mukherjee are shown as potential individuals who face the bitter truth of their lives as immigrant but do not fall prey to the circumstances rather they are strong enough to adapt themselves in the new environment .Tara is no exception.

Dimple Dasgupta in *Wife* strives to establish herself in the American culture is her quest for identity as an individual. The ghetto which surrounds Dimple seems to suffocate her because she totally wants to be free from the shackles of marriage. The marriage which gave hopes of freedom looks like bondage and to free her from this torture, she butchers her husband, Amit. She wishes to be more than what she was then and what she is now. She seems to be guileless in the fallacious world but her inner soul never leaves her free.

Human mind has to be compatible to change in order to maintain equanimity in life. Basic difference in U.S.A. is that life is full of mechanism and runs on the fast track and it stands counterpoised to the Indian life style. However any immigrant from different parts of the world is not at all in up taking and up keeping because it is a result of the split personality. The immigrants of the first generation for fear of losing their identity turns down to intermingle with the new culture that is to be endorsed. Although they maintain the same code of morals and decorum, they let the second generation merge into the new culture. Hence, it is possible for any woman to assimilate a new culture because the women are responsible for growing the next generation. Without fail, they are account for keeping up the culture code and traditions as they wish. Quite true, self – expression of Indian immigrant is a result of self – suppression. The modern society invites changes from the female characters. Any immigrant is subjected to adjust to any situation in a clever manner.

Tara's alienation is not only in Vassar but also she is marginalized in her own hometown creating havoc on her senses. It is too much difficult to face the expatriation in her home where she was brought up like a princess. She feels alienated in the company of her friends who treat her as an American born and bred in an Indian environment. Tara feels completely confused to embrace the foreign culture after her marriage.The state of Bharati Mukherjee that one change every moment has an essence of self – realized person. She blends the myth with reality to create an individual. It can be found in each of her characters whose minds are filled with negatives and positives. Never the novelist fails to authenticate widely diasporic experiences in her writing because the characters are on the surface of ghetto and diasporic existence. Some of her characters who are fickle minded become varied. But most of the female characters decide their own future and establish their identity tremendously.

Through their action, they not only revolutionize but also prove themselves to be adventurous to build up future life style in the New World as they are fully aware of their past mingling with the present to form their future. In fact, they are to transformations and new experiences by means of which they change themselves.

The freedom of expression and release from the traditional attitude make the protagonists of Bharati Mukherjee surge forward to be exuberant in their Americaness. The initial hesitant moves either through self-inflected violence as in Dimple's case in *Wife* or Violence from outside as in *The Tiger's Daughter* and in *Jasmine* pushes these individuals towards renunciation.

Themes of traditional transformations into self mutating heroines permeate the novels. It consecutively authenticates the theory of reinventing selves by rebirth. The heroines undergo pangs of rebirth to immense into the imperialistic America which strongly believes inn colonizing the immigrants and the aliens. Negating the notion of existing in the state of hypernation and hybridization Bharati Mukherjee establishes herself as a American writer. In order to balance between the beliefs of old culture which seems to be binding in the new environment and the new world which suffers new horizons to the enchained souls, the female protagonists take new course with their characterization.

Dimple in *wife* is unable to handle the pressure whereas Jasmine juggles through each new avenue with flourish. Although it is easy for Jasmine, she loses nothing. She enters the new world yet it does not have to grit to find a foothold for herself because she is always insecure and dependent on Amit Basu to offer freedom on the platter of marriage. When her husband fails to fulfil her fantasies, he becomes an adversary. Dimple, the protagonist never follows the virtues of the legendary wife. The heroine commits adultery to the surprise of all. However she tries to be a traditional wife.

Meanwhile her psyche induces her to be a rebel. Dimple, being one among the alienated characters has rootlessness and unreal existence. What she dreamt about the marriage is: Marriage would bring her freedom, cocktail parties on carpeted lawn fund raising dinners for noble charities. Marriage would bring her lover. On contrast, marriage gives an opportunity to Dimple to bring out her identity in the society. According to the suggestion, Dimple in *Wife* is in conflict of culture and comes out of the examination with flying colours to prove her identity for liberty.

Dimple has never been able to relate herself to her tradition or to her tradition to understand it. All her actions are geared towards the future and this bespeaks of the main problem: the utter rootlessness of her life... the sense of time as it exists in Mukherjee's novel is important for understanding of Dimple's life. The present and the past do not interact in *Wife*. There is questioning of the Indian situation of how do the past-independence generations relate to their own country, how they get post the colonial experience and free themselves from western attraction. For example, however, there seems to be on way out; the distance covered cannot be retraced she is an immigrant both in place and mind, has is the foreignness of spirit.

While female characters like Dimple Dasgupta survive and revise, they stay for a while between two worlds until they chose between two so as to find a space to inhabit. The new worlds in which they must interfere and negotiate hold a promise of the new selfhood and new battles against marginalization. Self-assertion alone urges them to enjoy further. Jasmine, the eponymous heroine of Bharati Mukherjee's new world takes an effective and impressive role. One could understand that the basic idea is self-empowerment which is essential for any human being.

'Kali' being an embodiment of empowered 'self', a mother, protector, slays the demons and wears the garland of severed heeds. Kali's anger is subdued only when she steps on her husband. Both signify the power of women and the intense rigor that is needed for a woman to have a life of her own. 'Goddess' is a term which protects idea that virtues are beyond the human race.

Although Bharati Mukherjee introduces the female protagonists in her novel, the male counterpart hardly come into any scene of novels. The novelist displays all types of temperaments in her work where one can find her working out the mental and physical interaction of female mind. Vividly the male counterparts are engaged as subordinated. The basic instinct of the male mind that is traditionally incubated is nothing but the feeling of superiority which the women aim eternity to break through their individual identity in the society in the modern society.

Characters undergo continuous process of transition. The transmigration not only covers but also exemplifies a vast periphery which is not purely national but transnational. Transition which is evident in each of her characters is her own self-portrayal in her characters, which face twists and turns, pros and cons, mishaps and pains. There are the intricacies where women delicately paint the right and make the readers feel painful. Which the immigrants sustain and inspire them to change their attitudinal problems and overcome hesitations so as to bring out their identity. Generally one sympathizes with each one of the characters, who struggle tooth and nail to create a new identity. Her protagonists rejuvenate in the new open atmosphere. Their exhilaration is infectious. Choice of being your own 'self' prevails over all the struggles and hurdles of life give out a new hope in their life.

One accepts the fact that the protagonist of her novels is mere shadows. Her novels can be said to be autobiographical. Her expressions are nothing but her deep rooted emotions. Murdering her own husband with little mercy by Dimple Dasgupta, she thinks is a release from a complicated life. Dimple is immersed with difficulties. The part of Amit Basu aggravates the situation. The catastrophe to Amit is a significant turning point for the women who like to bring out their identity. As for the Indian culture, women who fail to retaliate, succumb to their distress. In order to restore her emotions and release from commotions, she commits the crime. Success of Dimple's ultimate strife to establish herself in the American culture is her quest for identity as an individual. She moves away from the new world because of her gender limitations.

It is human beings' attitude that anybody will usually manifest unhappy feelings due to either detachment in the American society or new environment of the U.S.A. certainly lack of emotional attachment leads to hazardous consequences but excess of love smoothens the natural growth in the Indian culture. Hesitation with emotion and assimilation stand in Dimple in embracing the new culture and its ideologies which alone tend towards marginalization of 'self' and 'others'. The novel echoes the ideologies of Hinduism. But the American culture imbibes a different facet to the infiltration of the peripheries. Jasmine's life is transformed with the murder of the husband. Quest for 'self' to transformation with difference in each of the characters of Bharati Mukherjee is a great phenomenon.

Her characters rarely lose right of what Mukherjee calls very rightly their not-quietness. Through characterization, she brings into glimpse the psychic extremes and historical turmoil of India's present and past. Notwithstanding, they long for success and arability in their adopted homes, yet they are torn by the consequences of their new identities.

Each of Bharti Mukherjee's characters speaks for itself, be it major or minor or whatever it may be each one gives a new meaning to life. There is energy as well as force in their call and urge. Her characters reach beyond are real. Some of them are life-sized. The ethics governs the characters because it treats each of them individually and gives room to facilitate everyone's evolution.

Feminism in the characters of Bharati Mukherjee's is equipoise to make them vibrant and flamboyant. Each of the characters is treated as an individual. The power which exists inside the heart of each character is absolutely dominant at some point is forced out to make its presence felt. The passive existence of each character undergoes a dramatic change. The attitude of servility to treat men with veneration is evident in the traditional Indian patriarchal set up but the protagonists in each novel by the act of violence, self- mutation and transformation seem to be successful at their identity exposition. Themes of transnational transformations into that occur in the novels deals with the theories demystification of the identity. Transformation is quite mutual because America not only adjusts but also adapts to the strength that infiltrated the peripheries of the First World. From 1890 to 1970, it becomes an internationalized culture. A notable recurrent feature of Bharati Mukherjee's novel is that it describes the new-immigrant women who are forced to mutate, transforming themselves to become self-emancipated, self-confident members of the American Society. Brinda Bose opines to Tara (*The Tiger's daughter*, Dimple (*wife*) and jasmine continuing to be Indian, concentrate to being the kind of daughter, wife and widow that tradition demanded of them- decorous, submissive and loyal but it seemed highly incongruous in the contexts of their present lives, becoming an American presented the possibility of power to change their fates.

Women never like to be the traditional role models. They no longer reconcile the models to their circumstances. What drives them to react with violence is nothing but frustration, suppression, alienation and immigration. They need an urgent charge. Being not confined to the social and cultural patterns of the past, women vigorously intended to enter into the (present) new world to claim their right of identity.

To credit, the female protagonists of Bharati Mukherjee is a blend of modern and traditional qualities and they believe in creating their own 'universe' and they find success to demystify themselves in the universe but the protagonists of Bharati Mukherjee cannot be judged as immoral individuals who have affairs because it is not prevaricated in the American Culture.

Regarding isolation, alienation and frustration of the female protagonists of these novels, Tara, Dimple and Jasmine, these novels demonstrate the autobiographical element consequently leading towards a complex personality of un-belonging state of mind. Mukherjee's early novels *The Tiger's Daughter* and *Wife* explore the conditions of being Indian expartriates in the U.S.A. however, they are geographically and respectively expatriates in mind and spirit. According to the suggestion of Emmanuel Nelson, Mukherjee shows the diasporic Indian as living in between two cultures constantly journeying into new meanings and fashioning new identities.

It remains undenied, while focusing on the lives of characters that migrate to U.S.A., Mukherjee produces and provokes thinking over the cultural displacement as one terms the exuberant clash of immigrant cultures.

The novelist presents some of the most violent and grotesque aspects of cultural collisions. A close examination of her fiction reveals that the Western and Indian worlds give them an authentic and objective perspective with mixture of charm, and sympathy. They (worlds) push their protagonists to the edges of their worlds and liberate them for a new world order- demystifying their identity in the society because they aspire to come out of their turbulent mind. 'Third Space" designed by Bharati Mukherjee occupies in every cultural encounter. She admits that in her novels *The Tiger's Daughter* and *Wife* characters appear 'caught in a crisis situation'. Unless one considers the period and complexities of the cultural dynamics, no study about the immigrant culturalism can be done. Swami describes Dimple's "lacerated and anguished spirit" (*W*, 88). Similarly Imandar calls both Tara and Dimple as "the troubled spirits belonging nowhere in the end" (77). Both critics notify the luminal phase of disorder, disturbance and disorientation.

One is sure of the fact that the post colonialism starts with the animal of
the 'Third World'.

Disjunction and dislocation become a psychic pathology.it reflects an objective reality. Mukherjee looks at India from the perspective of third world writers, expatriates and immigrants. Her India figures in her narratives as a third world peace. Her protagonists cross geographical and psychological boundaries in an attempt to look for their roots remembering their ancestral ties with their homelands. On the top of it, her novels deal with nostalgia for a lost home, disillusionment of expatriation, fragmentation of the self, exuberance of immigration, assimilation, cultural translation and negotiation.

Tara the role of the protagonist is effective. She wants to lead a life. She is ambitious of keeping her identity. Although she is not satisfied with the Indians in Calcutta who treats her badly and loses identity with them, she is confident of constructing her individual identity of an Indian woman with her American husband in mind and sprit.in this connection she gets success. Her *The Tiger's Daughter* makes a new trend in fictional writings. In these novels, leaving their native country for an alien land is meant that liberating themselves from the clutches of a convention bound society.

Human relationships are fragile in these continents whether Europe or America. In India the human relations are stable to a large extent owing to the traditional virtues of the culture. Otherwise in the United States of America, Canada and other western countries, civilized matters tend to develop more in rational and materialistic way. Bharati Mukherjee's life and her transitions, her marriage to an American and her shift to Canada, her turbulent and sabbatical years turns her an immigrant. It stands for enjoying a pivotal moment in her life establishing her evolution as an individual and an author.

A notable recurrent feature of Mukherjee's novels is that these novels depict the new immigrant woman who is forced to mutate and transform themselves so as to become self emancipated self confident members of the American society. As for the male protagonists are concerned, they are left to dwindle between the two cultures and despite their patriarchal superiority, the female protagonists appear demeaned. Dimple in *Wife* and Jasmine in *Jasmine* more for India to America to be forced by violent action of self mutate. Ultimately with each transformation a new name is associated with the characters somehow or other sinister in essence mark the rebirth of each character. The novelist strongly believes in the Hinduism.

By fusing the philosophies of Hinduism and Buddhism into the structure of the novels, Mukherjee lays emphasis upon the fact that every death marks the new life. An oral teaching and clear narration about the Hindu mythological stories make their way into the plots of each novel, an just a position of traditional Hindu culture gives a new outlook to each of her novels.

Tara in *The Tiger's Daughter* seems to be more balanced due to her education in England. Her ideal person in life is none other than her father and so she always feels safe and secure with him. While in India she starts to forget all the details of her husband who is in a distant land, she loses her sanity under pressure. However, she decides to return to her husband and joins him to lead a peaceful life, exposing identity and enjoying her liberty all along. She is very strong in such confidence that will bring her credibility from the American.

Dimple in *Wife* forges her way into a new culture and wants to avoid her native identity whereas Tara Banerjee wants to return her home country so as to trace her own inherited identity. Only way of dimple in wife to freedom is by killing whereas for jasmine, in jasmine killing becomes necessary to maintain sanity. Jasmine takes revenge upon her rapist, reconciles and moves forward because the driving force before Jasmine to commit self-immolation. The intention is totally difficult because jasmine lives her husband enough to commit sati (self-immolation in the fire). Prakash molded her a life which was different from that of life which she had in her parent's house. Only confidence given by her husband makes her lead a balanced life because she has already faced the basic realities of life.

Dimple in *Wife* is unaware of the realities because throughout the novel she lives in a world of dream and fantasy. She withdraws herself from reality. Each character of Bharati Mukherjee is endowed with innate qualities of humanity and duality in personality. Each plot is integrated with factor that can be visible in reality of each character, concept of dualism is purely an ideology extracted from *The Vedas* and *Bhagavad Gita* where each and every person has a duality in everyone's personality: one which is meant for one's own 'self' and the other for behavioural attitude.

Bhagavad Gita is the greatest holy book of the Hindu and it has stored valuable doctrines that have influenced Bharati Mukherjee very much in her life. Dualism is a factor which exists in each and every mortal being and seems to be evident in each character (the protagonist) of Bharati Mukherjee be it Dimple, Jasmine, Hannah Easton or Devi or Tara. Thrown into psychedelic conditions, the female characters fight to get rooted and at the same time face the gender difference, the culture differences and the choices are theirs to make.

Jasmine would have reverted to her decision to commit suicide and after molestation, she behaved and did reasonably because her adoption, widow and remarriage, as for her as a village girl, are something alien, she is craving for surviving in the world and she thinks that she cannot leave with an unfinished business, emphasizing the philosophies of *The Holy Bhagavad Gita*. The sole ambition of Jasmine to self-immolate takes her to America where slays her rapist, adjusts with all types of all situations and conditions. She manages all with a brave heart, keeping her mind focused upon leading her life and possessing her own 'identity'. The 'Third Eye' signifies to opening of mind of knowledge as in Hinduism. Her marriage to Prakash leads her to transformation from a coarse village girl Jyoti into Jasmine.

Pygmalion was not a play I'd seen or read then but I realize how much professor Higgins there was in my husband. He wanted to break down the Jyoti I'd been in Hasanpur and make me a new kind of city woman. To break off the part, he gave me a new name: Jasmine. He said, "You are small and sweet and heady my Jasmine you'll quicken the whole world with your perfume. (*J*, 77)

Jasmine, the stone-hearted woman is supposed to forage through her destiny and keeps her deep-rooted to attain identity. She is guided by intuition and transformation. Each event is celebratory for her. She has little hassle in staying with Bud. She is pregnant with Bud's child but she leaves with Taylor to find new happiness. Neither hesitation non-tradition binds her at all. She flies to America which is a journey into flow of a peaceful life. Pleasure is hers, Jasmine who changes identities becomes victorious with every activity.

Basically and notably, the protagonists of Bharati Mukherjee's novels are a mixed bundle of Hindu feminism. Influences of incarnations of 'Sita' and 'Kali' come through forcefully into their beings.

Commonly anyone like these female characters who win the heart of the readers because of Mukherjee's characterization does not need to let go off their thoughts as well as beliefs but anyone can find changes in life which is the best and easiest way for a happy life. It is a philosophy of life: Bounce Forward each one of Bharati Mukherjee's characters seems to be precariously balanced on a right-nope in case they fall but they manage to travel pleasantly. In order to balance between the beliefs of old culture that binds in the new environment and the new world that show new horizons to these enchained 'souls' that expect a new course of life.

The fight to control 'self' to refrain and restrain the natural instincts of sensuality, dreams and expectations from marriage would not be much more difficult if they (the women characters live in India). In the event of facing America and its cosmopolitan society expedites the hunger in Dimple to refashion her 'self'. To raise voice to her suppressed feelings is not at all easy for her because the grooming of 'self' has been in rigid society which consider the act as an abhorrence and violence. The only way to gain freedom from the fight of duality (between her heart and mind) finds its way by stabbing her husband, Amit. She does and identity emerged successfully.

Mukherjee highlights the expansion of the identity during these cultural transactions and retains the collective identity through characterization. Characters of Bharati Mukherjee are constantly fighting in order to exist in a world of 'otherness.' The 'otherness' remains unlimited to the new culture of the new world but the constant fight is still vigorous within their own identity. Undoubtedly mutation triggers chain reaction within the soul of each character. The phenomenal problem of the female characters is nothing but "fighting within" because of the inevitable bonded position.

The postcolonial critics assert that Mukherjee yields to the hegemony of the west and therefore she tries to signify the importance of individuality. Mukherjee perceives the U.S.A. to be a land of challenging and promising in a stable condition wave one's individuality, liberty and identity. At the same time, she points India in the postcolonial society which prevents anybody else from fulfilling individuality. It is proved that identity is everyone's liberty of birthright.

Bharati Mukherjee sees America as the new world an account of the nano-technology, globalization, transculturation and cosmopolitanism. So, she claims to be an American writer of Indian origin, and her literary contribution brings a unique credit to the Indian woman novelist. Mukherjee is considered as an eminent specialist is diasporic experience and a good novelist in dealing with immigrant problems.

For both demystification and reconstruction of the immigrant character's identity, it needs a basis of the post-colonial theory which is closely integrated with literary studies. Pertaining to the vast scope of the post-colonial theory which has both thought and energy which make the human beings attains experience and awareness in life irrespective of caste, creed, religion and nationality.

Although the woman-novelists pitch their voice for social dignity and liberal liberty and enrich the multi-culturalism, they concentrate on the importance of the female identity in the society.. Cultural alienation is a world phenomenon today. The tremendous difference between two ways of life leads a person to a feeling of depression and frustration. This could be called "Culture Shock" when a person leaves his own culture and enters another; his old values come into conflicts with the new one he finds. The major literary works of Bharati Mukherjee have highlighted the immigrant anxiety. She invariably focuses upon sensitive women protagonists who lack firm sense of cultural identity and are natural victims of racisms, sexism and numerous forms of social oppression. The theme Bharati Mukherjee deals with in her novels is one of the significant themes of modern literature that is the depiction of cultural clash causing cultural and psychological conflicts. The subject has no doubt assumed great significance in the present world of globalization. Cross-cultural confrontation has received a pronounced impetus since the emergence of the modernist movement in the very opening of the 20th century. The globalization of world economy can be looked upon as a natural offshoot of multiculturalism and intercultural interaction. Bharati Mukherjee has been widely acknowledged as voice of expatriate-immigrant sensibility. Hence the subject has assumed national and international status.

All human beings adopt their mother culture so that it becomes their identity. Immigration poses a new dilemma of cultural identity. There starts a cultural conflict between mother culture and adopted culture. Consequently this process leads to psychological crisis. Bharati Mukherjee's fictional world of women immigrants presents the traumatic experiences in the process of expatriation to immigration. Her women protagonists consequently suffer from sense of alienation, identity crisis, cultural shock and a consequent psychological conflict.

Bibliography

Mukherjee, Bharati. *Jasmine.* New York: Grove, 1989. Print.

Mukherjee, Bharati. *The Tiger's Daughter.* Canada: Ballantine Books, 1992. Print.

Mukherjee, Bharati. *Wife.* Canada: Ballantine Books, 1992. Print.

9 798889 590224

Printed by Libri Plureos GmbH in Hamburg,
Germany